ENDANGERED!

WHALES

Amanda Harman

Series Consultant: James G. Doherty
General Curator, The Bronx Zoo, New York

BENCHMARK BOOKS

MARSHALL CAVENDISH

NEW YORK

Benchmark Books
Marshall Cavendish Corporation
99 White Plains Road
Tarrytown, New York 10591-9001

Library of Congress Cataloging-in-Publication Data

Harman, Amanda, 1968-
    Whales / by Amanda Harman.
        p.   cm. — (Endangered!)
    Includes bibliographical references (p.   ).
    Summary: Explores how whales live, why they are in danger, and
what is being done to stop them from disappearing from our planet
forever.
    ISBN 0-7614-0219-5 (lib. bdg.)
    1. Whales—Juvenile literature.   2. Endangered species—Juvenile
literature.   [1. Whales. 2. Endangered species.]   I. Title.
II. Series.
QL737.C4H27 1996
599.5—dc20   95-48172
                                                         CIP
                                                          AC

Printed in Hong Kong

PICTURE CREDITS
*The publishers would like to thank the Frank Lane Picture Agency (FLPA) for
supplying all the photographs except for the following:* Ardea 1, 24; Bruce
Coleman Ltd 6, 9, 17, 20, 28; T. Johnson/Earthviews/FLPA 12; Panda/FLPA
18, 22; Richard Sears/Earthviews/FLPA 8; Sunset/FLPA 4, 7, 25; James
Watt/Earthviews/FLPA 16.

Series created by Brown Packaging

Front cover: Humpback whale.
Title page: Gray whale.
Back cover: Belugas.

Contents

Introduction

Whales are among the biggest animals that have ever lived on Earth. As they cruise beneath the ocean like living submarines or burst suddenly from the water in a cloud of spray, they are awesome and spectacular creatures.

You might think that whales are some kind of giant fish, since they live in the ocean. But they are not fish; they belong to a large group of animals called **mammals** that includes bears, monkeys, and human beings among others. Mammals usually have hair or fur on their bodies. Over

Whales sometimes leap out of the water. These are humpback whales and can be recognized by their long flippers.

millions of years, whales have lost most of their hair, except for a few bristles on their head. This has made their skin smoother and their bodies more streamlined so that they can swim easily through the water. Without the warmth of hair, however, whales would soon get very cold in the dark ocean depths. So they have a layer of fat under their skin to keep them warm. This fat is called blubber.

Whales have **adapted** in other ways to living in the sea. Their bodies are shaped like torpedoes, and they have flippers instead of arms. Their huge, paddle-like tails push them forward when they swim. However, unlike fish, whales cannot breathe underwater and must come to the surface regularly to gulp fresh air. They draw in air through a special "blowhole" on the top of their head. As a whale

The tail of a gray whale breaks the surface of the water. Whales' tails are flat, unlike those of most fish, which are upright.

reaches the surface of the water, it breathes out before it breathes in again. Its breath is forced out of the blowhole in a huge powerful puff called a "blow." When the weather is cold, the blow forms a cloud just as human breath does and can be seen several miles away.

Whales belong to the group of mammals known as **cetaceans** (si-TAY-shuns). There are about 80 different **species** of cetaceans, including about 40 kinds of dolphins and porpoises, which are whales' smaller cousins. Whales live in all the world's oceans, from the warm waters near the Equator to the freezing waters around the poles.

Scientists believe that whales used to live on land, but moved into the sea millions of years ago. Since then, many species of whales have existed. Some of these are now

A right whale breathes out. Some whales have one blowhole; others, like right whales, have two.

extinct because they could not get used to changes in the environment. Sadly, many species of whales alive today are in danger of becoming extinct, too. They are threatened not by nature but by human contact. For hundreds of years, people hunted the largest whales for their meat, blubber, oil, and bones, until some species were almost wiped out. Humans have also put many species of whales at risk by **polluting** the oceans with garbage and chemicals.

Whales are divided into two main types: baleen (buh-LEEN) whales and toothed whales. In this book we will look at both of them. We will find out how they live, why they are in danger, and what is being done to stop them from disappearing from our planet forever.

A beluga pokes its head out of the water. Unlike their giant relatives, these small whales are kept in a number of marine aquariums.

Baleen Whales

Baleen whales have huge "curtains" of bristles hanging from the roof of their mouth. These take the place of teeth and are made of a horny, elastic substance called baleen, from which these whales got their name. Also known as "whalebone", baleen is similar to the material that our fingernails are made of. Experts cannot agree on how many species of baleen whales exist, but there are about ten. We will look at five here: the blue whale, the gray whale, the humpback whale, and the two species of right whales.

So how do these enormous animals eat if they have no teeth? Baleen whales do not need teeth, because they have a special way of feeding, called filter feeding. They live on

Baleen whales differ greatly in shape. The blue whale (pictured here) is slender, whereas right whales are heavy-set.

small fish and **plankton** (tiny animals and plants that live in the sea in huge numbers), especially very small, shrimplike creatures called krill. Krill often live together in vast clouds in the water, turning the sea into a kind of "krill soup." To feed, most baleen whales take in large mouthfuls of krill-filled seawater. After each gulp, they use their massive tongue to push the water back out through the tiny gaps between the bristles, leaving behind a mouthful of krill to swallow. In this way, the whales use the curtains of baleen plates in their mouth like a huge sieve.

Some baleen whales feed by swimming slowly through the masses of krill with their mouth wide open, only swallowing now and then when they have gathered a large

A right whale swims with its mouth open, showing its curtains of light-colored baleen. Right whales are up to about 55 feet (17 m) long and can weigh as much as 80 tons.

amount of food. The right whales feed in this way. Others, such as the blue whale, prefer to lunge into the krill soup to get a large mouthful at one time.

The humpback whale also feeds by lunging. And it has an amazing way of gathering its food into one place so that it can take in as much as possible in one mouthful. The humpback actually captures its food by surrounding it with a net of bubbles! Whenever the whale spies a school of fish or krill swimming through the water, it swims around and around in a circle beneath it, blowing out bubbles of air all the while. The bubbles surround its **prey**, which is afraid to pass through them. The humpback then lunges through the

Humpbacks feed by lunging through large masses of prey. The mouth and throat of the whale on the right are swollen with water and food.

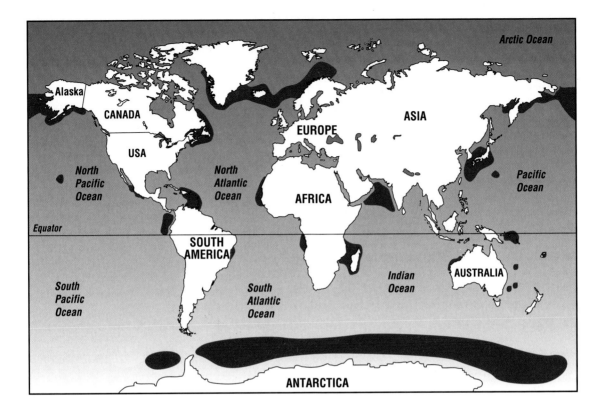

Areas where the
humpback whale
can be found

mass of creatures with its mouth open, taking in huge
amounts of water and food.

The humpback belongs to a group of baleen whales
known as rorquals (RAW-kwuhls). Rorquals have up to 100
long grooves from the chin down to the belly. These pleats
allow the whales to stretch their skin and swell up like a
balloon when they suck in water and food. The humpback
is found in all the world's oceans, in both cold and warm
waters. There were once about 150,000 humpbacks, but
whaling has reduced this number to just 25,000.

The gray whale feeds in a slightly different way from
other baleen whales. It has shorter, thicker baleen plates
than the others do and lives in the shallow seas just off the
coast instead of in the open ocean. It is perfectly adapted

for feeding on the seabed, where its swims on its side, plowing its head through the sand. It uses its baleen bristles like large combs to pick up small sea creatures, such as fish and crabs. Gray whales once lived in the Atlantic and Pacific oceans, but the Atlantic whales were hunted to extinction in the seventeenth century. Scientists think that about 21,000 gray whales survive in the Pacific Ocean, along the east coast of northern Asia and the west coast of North America.

The biggest whale of all is the blue whale, which can grow to almost 100 feet (30 m) long and can weigh a massive 160 tons. This is not only the largest whale, but the largest animal ever to have lived on Earth – even bigger than the biggest dinosaur! The blue whale is still found in all the oceans of the world, although it is highly

A gray whale takes a look at what is going on above the surface. See how much shorter its bristles are than those of the right whale on page 9.

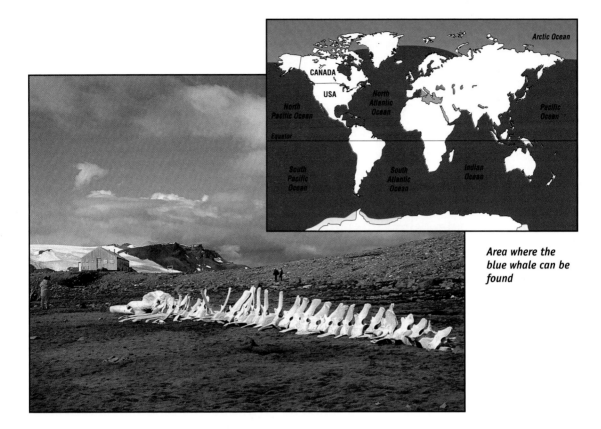

Area where the blue whale can be found

endangered. As the largest whale, it was much prized by whalers. Once there were about 250,000; now it is thought that fewer than 15,000 are left in the northern half of the world and only a few hundred in the southern half.

The right whales were also favorite prey of whalers. In fact, they were named by whalers who called them the "right" whales to hunt. Most kinds of whales sank when they died, but the right whales floated, making them easier to catch. The reason the right whales stayed afloat was that they had so much blubber – up to 28 inches (70 cm) thick in places. There are two species of right whales: the southern right whale and the northern right whale. The northern right whale is the most endangered whale of all.

A blue whale skeleton lies near a closed-down whaling station in the Antarctic. Blue whales were heavily hunted. In the 1930s, almost 30,000 were once caught in a single year.

Baleen Whales

There are probably only about 350 left in the world, and this number does not seem to be getting any bigger.

Whales – both baleen and toothed – usually breed every two years. In order to **mate**, males first need to find a partner. This is not easy, since whales are often separated by great distances in the open seas. The male humpback whale, for example, "sings" to attract a female. His long, complicated songs usually last up to half an hour, and other whales can hear them underwater from more than 100 miles (160 km) away. One humpback whale, whose singing was recorded by scientists, sang for more than 24 hours without stopping.

Areas where the northern right whale (red) and southern right whale (brown) can be found

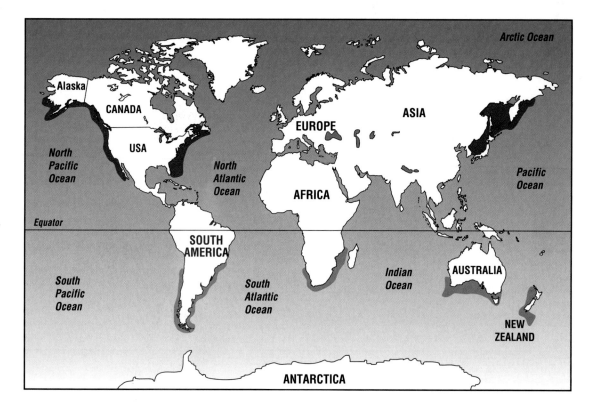

Areas where the gray whale can be found

Humpbacks are also famous for leaping high into the air above the water and diving back in with a huge splash. This is known as "breaching." Scientists are not sure why whales do this. When males breach, they may be trying to attract females or perhaps to scare away rival males.

Between 12 and 18 months after mating (depending on the species), the female gives birth to a single baby, known as a calf. Whale calves are fairly well developed when they are born. A newborn blue whale weighs several tons and measures 22 feet (6.7 m) from head to tail! The baby can

Not only humpbacks breach. Here a gray whale leaps from the water in the San Ignacio Lagoon, Baja California.

swim immediately, but it stays close to its mother for the first few weeks, almost clinging to her as it travels along beneath her belly or near the fin on her back. It feeds on its mother's milk. This is very nutritious, and the young whale grows at a fast rate – almost 2 inches (5 cm) a day. Calves drink their mothers' milk for between six months and two years, depending on the species.

Some baleen whales spend the summer in **temperate** and cold waters, because that is where the most plankton is found. Before winter comes, however, the whales set off on a long journey to warmer waters near the Equator. Females give birth to their calves during the winter and if they did

A humpback and calf swim together. A humpback is about 14 feet (4.3 m) long at birth. Fully grown it will be about 53 feet (16 m) long and weigh up to 40 tons.

this in the freezing waters of the Arctic and Antarctic, their babies would never survive. As winter draws to a close, the whales return once again to colder waters. This kind of yearly journey is called a **migration**.

One of the most familiar whale migrations is that of the gray whale. This is because eastern Pacific whales have a route that takes them very close to the North American shore, where thousands of tourists gather to watch them on their way every year. In September or October, the whales set out from their feeding grounds in Alaska and swim all the way down to Mexico. Swimming up to 110 miles (175 km) a day, they reach Baja California in December. Just two months later, in February, they are on their way back to Alaska. This time, they have newborn calves with them, so they cover only about 50 miles (80 km) a day.

Gray whales at sea. Female grays are usually slightly bigger than males. On average, female grays are about 45 feet (14 m) long and weigh up to 35 tons.

Toothed Whales

Toothed whales, as their name suggests, have teeth and not baleen plates. There are about 30 different species of them, including beaked whales and bottlenose whales. Here we will concentrate on just three toothed whales that are in great danger: the sperm whale, the beluga, and the narwhal.

The sperm whale is the biggest of all the toothed whales. A male sperm whale may grow to almost 70 feet (21 m) long from head to tail and weigh nearly 60 tons. The females are much smaller than this, however. They grow no bigger than 45 feet (14 m) and weigh about 20 tons.

This young sperm whale has fish, called remoras, attached to it. They do the whale no harm but eat the lice that live on its thick skin.

The sperm whale is easy to recognize by its huge, squared head, which is as big as a car. Inside this head are two very important things. First, it houses the largest brain of any animal in the world, which can weigh as much as 20 pounds (9 kg). Second, it is full of thick, waxy oil.

Unfortunately for the sperm whale, people valued this oil very highly since they could use it in a number of products, including ointments and women's cosmetics. Because of this, the sperm whale was at one time the most hunted of all whales. In just one year – 1963 – more than 35,000 sperm whales were caught and killed by whalers. Today, some sperm whales still survive in all the oceans of

Areas where the sperm whale can be found

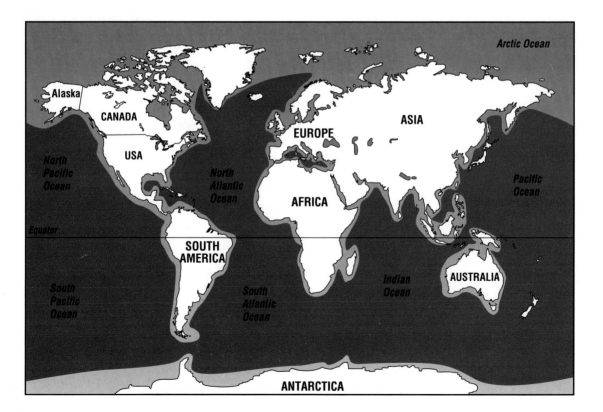

the world. Females and their babies usually stay in the warm waters around the Equator, while males can be found anywhere from the Equator to the poles.

The beluga and the narwhal are classed together in a subgroup called "white whales." The beluga lives up to this name: adults are a brilliant white. This helps to keep them hidden against the snow and ice when they come to the surface in the cold Arctic waters in which they live.

Narwhals also live in Arctic waters but are less strikingly colored than the beluga. Despite being called a white whale, the narwhal is actually covered with splotches of gray-green, black, and cream. Both the beluga and the

Belugas are reddish brown when they are born and change to gray when they are one year old. They become pure, bright white only when they reach adulthood.

narwhal are much smaller than the sperm whale, growing to about 16 feet (5 m) long and weighing just over 1.5 tons. In both species, the male is slightly larger than the female.

Having teeth means that toothed whales can feed on fish and squid, larger prey than the krill usually eaten by baleen whales. Unlike many other meat-eating animals, though, toothed whales do not have long, sharp teeth for ripping up their food. They swallow their prey whole, and their teeth are usually fairly flat and worn down. They seem to be used for grabbing rather than chewing food.

The sperm whale has between 40 and 50 teeth. They are some of the biggest teeth of any animal on Earth, and most

Areas where the beluga can be found

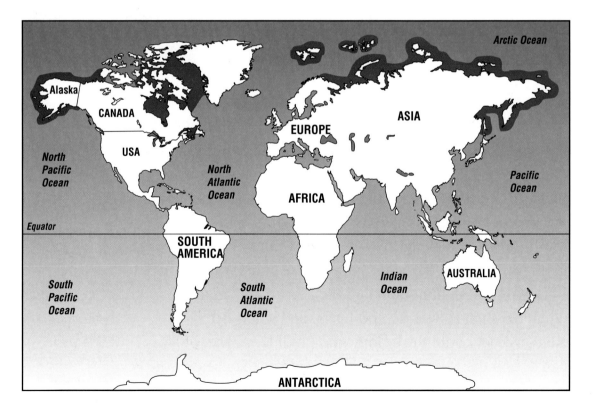

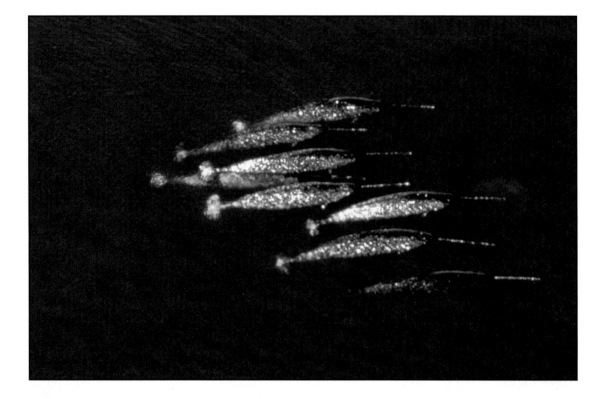

of them are found in the whale's lower jaw. Narwhals, on the other hand, have only two teeth, one on either side of the upper jaw. In males, once the teeth reach about 8 inches (20 cm) in length, the right one stops growing. But the left tooth keeps on getting longer, spiraling forward until it forms a tusk up to 10 feet (3 m) long. This tusk has given the narwhal its other name of "sea unicorn."

Belugas often hunt alone on the seabed for small creatures such as worms, mollusks, and small fish. Belugas' necks are fairly long and flexible, so the whales can sweep their heads from side to side as they search the bottom. It is more difficult to catch fish and other creatures

Narwhals photographed from the air. The male narwhal's tusk is probably for attracting females and fighting with other males at breeding time. It is not used for eating.

that swim in the open sea, and belugas usually hunt this kind of prey in small groups. The belugas work together to "herd" the fish, trapping them in shallow water, where they can catch them more easily.

Besides fish such as cod and flounder, narwhals hunt shrimp and small squid and octopus. Sperm whales hunt even larger prey, including sharks and giant squid. Giant squid can be 50 feet (15 m) long or more, including their tentacles, and they often put up a fierce fight. Sperm whales have been found with huge scars on their heads made by the suckers on these tentacles. When searching for giant squid, sperm whales often dive very deep.

Areas where the narwhal can be found

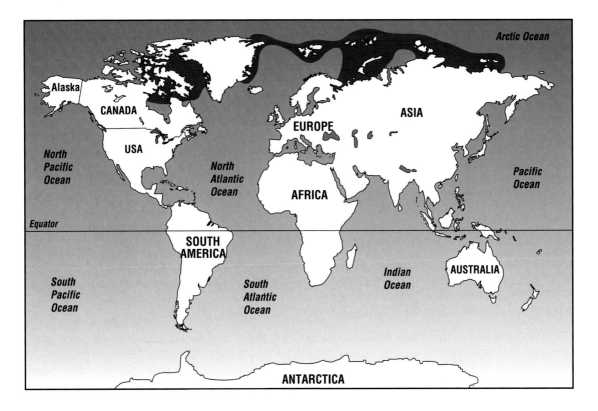

Most whales have a very poor sense of smell but can see fairly well. Their best sense, though, is their hearing. Toothed whales also use a special skill called **echolocation**. The whale sends out a series of sounds, which spread through the water and bounce back off anything solid that they strike. The whale receives the echoes and can tell where the animal or object is in the water and how big it is. Echolocation is particularly important for toothed whales in search of prey. Baleen whales may also be able to use echolocation, but scientists are not sure.

Unlike baleen whales, which spend most of their time alone, toothed whales are sociable animals. Many species, including the beluga, narwhal, and sperm whale, swim together in groups called **pods**. Each pod is usually made up of either young males or females with their babies.

A diver swims with a sperm whale. These animals can easily outdive humans – and they don't need breathing equipment. One male regularly dove to 10,500 feet (3200 m), staying underwater for one to two hours!

Members of a pod communicate with one another through a wide range of noises, including clicks, chirps, and whistles. Belugas are particularly noisy. Whalers used to call them "sea canaries" because their sounds reminded them of singing birds.

Toothed whales are very caring toward other members of their pod. If one of them becomes ill or is injured, the others soon come along to offer comfort or help. Sperm whales will arrange themselves in a circle around the sick or injured whale to protect it from further danger. However, whalers soon learned that if they injured one sperm whale, the others in its pod would gather around. The whalers could then kill them one by one.

The bump on the beluga's head is called a "melon." Experts believe it contains a special organ used in echolocation.

A whaling station in Iceland. In countries where whaling continues, whales are sometimes brought to places like this to be cut up after they have been killed at sea.

Saving Whales

People have endangered many species of whales. Pollution is a serious threat for whales, particularly for those that live near the coast. Large amounts of dangerous chemicals from factories and farms, as well as human waste from sewage plants are flushed into coastal waters each year. Fish and other marine animals take in these poisonous materials with their food. Whales then eat these creatures and become poisoned. Many countries have now agreed to control the amount of pollution they cause so that the oceans do not become too dirty for whales and other sea creatures to live in. Coastal whales are also at risk from ships. A number of belugas, which sometimes live in rivers and river mouths, have been run down and killed by ships in the Gulf of St Lawrence. Scientists fear that drilling for oil along the coast of Alaska may also harm these whales, as may building dams on rivers where belugas give birth.

But the main reason that whale numbers have dropped over the years is whaling. By the early twentieth century, whalers had killed so many of the largest species that they were running out of whales to catch. In 1946, an organization called the International Whaling Commission

This sperm whale died after becoming stuck on a beach. Whales sometimes lose their way and get stranded. They die unless people are there to help them back into the water.

Saving Whales

(IWC) was set up to control whaling. The IWC put a complete ban on hunting gray whales and right whales, and on killing humpback whales in the Antarctic. In the case of the remaining species of whales, the IWC gradually reduced the numbers that whalers were allowed to catch.

However, whales kept dying, and **conservationists** started to warn that whales were in danger of becoming extinct. People became worried and began to speak out against whale hunting. Finally, in 1986, the IWC banned large-scale whaling altogether for a time in an effort to save

Tourists meet a gray whale. People all over the world are now interested in whales, and "whale watching" has become very popular.

whales from disappearing altogether. A few whaling countries decided to keep on hunting in spite of the IWC ban. They agreed to reduce how many whales they took, but sadly hundreds of whales are still caught each year.

Even so, the future for whales now looks a little brighter. Whaling has not started again on a large scale, and in 1994 the IWC stated that the Antarctic should be set aside as a protected area for whales. Also, people have become interested in whales and do not want to see these animals disappear forever. It is too early to take whales off the danger list. But if there is no more large-scale hunting, and pollution can be controlled, these huge, mysterious animals may still glide through the oceans of tomorrow.

A humpback whale comes up for air. These whales can easily live for more than 20 years. And experts believe that one whale found off Australia may have been 48 years old!

Useful Addresses

For more information about whales and how you can help protect them, contact these organizations:

Cousteau Society
930 W. 21st Street
Norfolk, VA 23517

Greenpeace USA
1436 U Street NW
Washington, D.C. 20039

Save the Whales
Animal Welfare Institute
P.O. Box 3650
Washington, D.C. 20007

U.S. Fish and Wildlife Service
Endangered Species and Habitat
Conservation
400 Arlington Square
18th and C Streets NW
Washington, D.C. 20240

Whale Adoption Project
70 E. Falmouth Highway
East Falmouth, MA 02536

World Wildlife Fund
1250 24th Street NW
Washington, D.C. 20037

World Wildlife Fund Canada
90 Eglinton Avenue East
Suite 504
Toronto
Ontario M4P 2Z7

Further Reading

Endangered Wildlife of the World (New York: Marshall Cavendish Corporation, 1993)

Great Whales, the Gentle Giants Patricia Lauber (New York: Henry Holt, 1991)

The Sea World Book of Whales Eve Bunting (San Diego: Harcourt, 1988)

The Whale: The Sovereign of the Sea Caroline Brett (Garrett Educational Corp., 1992)

Whales Norman Barrett (New York: Franklin Watts, 1989)

Whales, Dolphins and Porpoises Mark Carwardine (New York: Dorling Kindersley, 1992)

Why Are the Whales Vanishing? Isaac Asimov (Milwaukee: Gareth Stevens, 1992)

Wildlife of the World (New York: Marshall Cavendish Corporation, 1994)

Glossary

Adapt: To change in order to survive in new conditions.

Cetacean (Si-TAY-shun): A marine mammal that breathes through a blowhole and has flippers and a powerful, flat tail. Whales, dolphins, and porpoises are all cetaceans.

Conservationist (Kon-ser-VAY-shun-ist): A person who protects and preserves the Earth's natural resources, such as animals, plants, and soil.

Echolocation (Ek-o-lo-KAY-shun): The skill that toothed whales use to find objects underwater. The whale sends out a sound. The sound waves travel until they strike an object. Then they bounce back, or echo, to the whale. When the whale receives this sound, it can tell how big the object is and where it is in the water.

Extinct (Ex-TINKT): No longer living anywhere in the world.

Mammal: A kind of animal that is warm-blooded and has a backbone. Most are covered with fur or have hair. Females have glands that produce milk to feed their young.

Mate: When a male and female get together to produce young.

Migration: A journey made regularly by some animals, usually from their home to their breeding area and back.

Plankton: The general name for many kinds of tiny plants and animals that live in water, often in large numbers.

Pod: The name given to a group of toothed whales.

Pollute (Puh-LOOT): To release damaging materials, such as garbage, fumes, and chemicals, into the environment.

Prey: An animal that is hunted and eaten by another animal.

Species: A kind of animal or plant. For example, the beluga is a species of whale.

Temperate: Neither very hot nor very cold. For example, temperate waters.

Index